FUNDAMENTALS

OF

GROUP

TREATMENT

FUNDAMENTALS

OF

GROUP

TREATMENT

BARUCH LEVINE

Assistant Professor
School of Social Service Administration
The University of Chicago

Publishers/WHITEHALL COMPANY/Chicago
320 W. Adams/Chicago, Ill

Many thanks to

James Friend,

Rachel B. Marks,

Bernece K. Simon,

and Mary Louise Somers

for their help in preparing this document.

FOREWORD

There is a clear and present need for this volume addressed to social caseworkers. Casework agencies all over the country are either interested in the possibilities of group treatment or embarked on exploratory projects testing group treatment as an important adjunct of individual treatment. Agency administrative personnel and social casework practitioners responsibly struggle with the question of the caseworker's professional competence to undertake group treatment. There is no doubt that, in addition to the help this book can offer, caseworkers need to study primary sources for the theory relating to groups, need to have competent social group work consultation and to devise ways for analysis and evaluation of their practice with groups. The study and work and spirit of adventure necessary to undertake group treatment can be facilitated and motivated by the content of Mr. Levine's work.

There is, here, a combination, in good balance of theory, principles and the "how-to" of implementation of both, in undertaking group treatment. Mr. Levine achieves this balance by presentation of concepts and principles followed by detailed discussion of examples of implementation.

FOREWORD

Mr. Levine is well-suited to have written this book. He has been both a social casework and social group work practitioner. In his advanced study, he had work in social casework theory and practice and he has and is acting as a social group work consultant to social caseworkers involved in group treatment. Most of Mr. Levine's experience has been in psychiatric facilities and much of the material in this book is based on that experience. The level of the presentation of concepts, principles and examples makes Mr. Levine's material readily applicable to most settings of social casework practice. It is a good introduction to a new venture in practice.

Bernece K. Simon
Professor and Director
Field Instruction
School of Social Service Administration
The University of Chicago

TABLE OF CONTENTS

CONTENTS

FUNDAMENTALS OF GROUP TREATMENT

INTRODUCTION

The principles within this work will provide a structure which caseworkers may readily use, first to develop
a purposeful orientation toward work with groups and
secondly to evaluate their own experiences. As workers
bring their own levels of social work knowledge and
skill to the use of this structure, they will find their own
ways of using the content.

In my consultations with caseworkers, I have found
that certain recurrent problems come up with regard to
work with treatment groups. From these problems and
from the possible solutions to them, emphasis on *clarity
of purpose* has become central. The purpose for which
any group has been formed influences all that follows.
Principles presented here represent a functional integration of theories from the study of small-group behavior,
the methods of social group work, and the methods and
goals of social casework treatment. Caseworkers may
thus use these principles to organize their own knowledge
and skills in ways that will facilitate their work with

their treatment groups.

Group treatment begins with the detection of need for services which can be implemented within and through a small group. It continues through the organization of service, intake process, the stages and sequence of treatment development, and the termination of group services within appropriate timing. Workers who employ this framework by starting with the formulation of purpose will find that during group meetings they are better able to evaluate what is happening and to determine what action to take.

Purposive action by social workers is critical in their work with groups. Individual and interpersonal behaviors and their possible implications become overwhelming unless the worker has a guide which will assist him in determining what is most suitable for response and what will be left alone. The task of group work without the guidance of purposes often results in the worker trying to treat everything at once or doing little if anything at all. Lack of purpose may also lead to the development of treatment techniques which are situationally determined, possibly inconsistent from one situation to another, or more protective of the worker than helpful to the group.

Clarity about the purpose for which the group is formed provides a framework for observation, assessment, and action. It facilitates the worker's ability to deal with the immediate situation in ways that are relevant to the achievement of treatment goals. With this purposeful orientation, the worker may become better able to make professional decisions based on conscious priorities rather than on pure intuition.

Clarity of purpose provides a base for the group members to develop a bond and a means for attaining their common goals. Without regard to purpose in the establishment of groups, there is increased danger of the groups' being weakened by basic interpersonal conflict which may sap energies from goal achievement. Although it is one of the major dynamics contributing to group growth and assistance to its members, conflict cannot be beneficial unless there is some combining of individual energies toward resolution. This combination of energies and its direction is called the vector of group energies or synergy. The principles centering on clarity of purpose in group work treatment are designed to facilitate the development of combined and directed energies toward the attainment of group goals. A purposeful orientation, or lack of it, may make the difference between a self-dependent, goal-striving group and a group waiting to be moved by the worker. The difference is similar to that between an individual client who is *engaged* in the treatment process and one who is a passive participant.

I. PURPOSE: CORE OF THE GROUP TREATMENT PROCESS

Purpose is the core of group function and *the ideal method for selecting a purpose for a social work treatment group is to begin with the identification of common needs among individuals in an agency or worker caseload.* This ideal is simply the basic social work approach of beginning with the detection of need. In the case of a potential group service, the need should be common to all the prospective members.

When the agency develops its purpose for establishing a group on the basis of detected common needs among individuals in a caseload, there is some assurance that the purposes of individual members for joining the group will be similar and in harmony with that agency purpose. A confluence of the purposes of the agency and individual members later develops into a dynamic group purpose through the group treatment process. The result is a healthy alignment of the three major kinds of purposes—the agency's, individual group member's, and group's. This alignment of purposes is the foundation of sound group treatment in accordance with social work objectives. Group purpose becomes a source for both the energy and the focus of the group effort. The worker can then help the group to use its energies to focus on solving problems. A confluence can be facilitated through groups formed by the agency in the manner just described. However, in natural groups, the worker may not be able to begin with an easily detected and common need. Natural groups are usually already formed when a worker is first contacted. Typical of these groups are the family, the adolescent gang, or even a long-standing friendship group in a psychiatric ward.

If a worker is to treat a natural group, the problem of aligning agency, member, and group purposes becomes more complex. The worker must concentrate on helping group members articulate their individual purposes along with their thoughts and feelings about them. Once this is accomplished, the problem becomes one of examining these individual purposes in order to ascertain whether or not they are common to the group as a whole. If they are, then the group is on its way to problem-solving. If, however, there is evidence of a disparity among the individual purposes, mutual accomodation or compromise will need to be worked out. In some instances, the group will be hopelessly divided into purpose factions, and work with the total group at the same time will be virtually impossible. If a group having divergent purposes among the members decides to continue working together, group interaction must always be viewed through the framework of this divergence.

Examples of Common and Divergent Purposes

Preparation for homemaking (common purpose). —
A caseworker in a psychiatric hospital detected that six
women in her in-patient caseload were facing the prospect
of returning to their roles as wife, mother, and homemaker. Difficulties arising from these particular roles had
contributed to or were manifestations of their psychiatric
illness. The worker decided that, because of the commonalities in their situations, the prospective members could
be helped toward finding more effective ways of coping
with their problems in a treatment group. While there
were other divergent elements to many of their individual
problems, the worker decided that their role demands
were significant and appropriate for social work help.

The members of the group all welcomed the prospect
of the proposed group. Once the meetings began, the
members found that they were easily able to identify with
one another because of the many similarities in their
individual situations. Some of the similarities were feelings of being trapped by loss of freedom, guilt over anger
at their children, constant fatigue, and unsureness of their
own and others' expectations for them in their respective
roles. As the group progressed, the members helped one
another consider ways of gratifying more of their own
needs.

PURPOSE

Preparation for retirement (common purpose). —
A worker detected a number of in-patient men and women
who came to the hospital because of problems asso-
ciated with late life adjustment. Generally these were
persons who had been active either in the home or at
their jobs until either they themselves or someone else
determined that they were unable to continue their re-
sponsibilities. Some major common concerns in this
group were the acceptance of dependency on others and
finding ways to enjoy their retirement years. These common concerns included consideration of what they could
do for themselves and the use of the facilities available
to them in the community.

Many groups in psychiatric hospitals center around
finding and holding jobs and relationships in the social
environment to which the patients will be returning.
Post-discharge groups are often formed on the same basis
of on-going support to patients while in the community.
With goals and purposes firmly established, the danger
of interminable dependency of the members on the group
is reduced since there will come a time when most or all
of the members can feel that they have utilized the group
experience as a bridge to on-going experiences on their
own.

Women's pre-discharge group (divergent purposes).
A worker in a psychiatric hospital established a pre-discharge group for the women in his ward. Half the group members were returning to their former social situations; the other half were going out to new surroundings under a family-care program. In the early stages, the group did well by focusing on the general motives and resistances to leaving the hospital. As the group progressed, the particular nature of the discharge became more important. The feeling of the members for one another sustained the group through a period of alternating discussion of the two circumstances, but the worker came to the conclusion that it would be more productive to split the group and in subsequent groups use one particular disposition as a criterion for grouping.

Relatives' groups — With relatives of patients it is well to keep in mind some of the distinctions that have been found to make a difference in purposes. Spouses and parents of patients have different problems to work out in relation to the patient. One usual distinction is that spouses are often attempting to improve and become closer in their relationship with the patients. Parents of adult or young adult patients usually aim at improving and at the same time becoming more distant in their relationship with the patient. Parents of child patients are aiming at improving their relationship with the patient, which differs in accordance with how long it may be anticipated that the patient must remain with the parents. Husbands and wives often have many different kinds of problems in adjusting to a marital relationship. One very practical thing to bear in mind is that there is only so much time and energy which a worker and his group members can put into a series of meetings. If the purpose and needs are too divergent, part of the group will be "in limbo" while other parts will be solving their problems, or becoming coworkers with the worker in helping with problems that have little meaning for them.

The most desirable type of group engagement occurs when discussion of someone else's problem has direct and significant meaning for each member in his own problem solving. Members then become co-problemed people helping each other instead of co-leaders intellectually dealing with somebody else's problem. This may be one difference between individual treatment in front of other people in the group meeting and group treatment.

A case can be made for a range of purposes consistent with social work services. My own rule of thumb is that, however, identified, the purpose of the group should be one that makes a difference to all the group members and one that is within the usual function of the agency-worker to be engaged with clients. If the group members do not really care about the purpose of the group then the result will be a loss of the purpose as the dynamic factor in group formation and goal production. If the purpose is one with which the worker is not familiar then he must familiarize himself with it at the same time he begins to learn about work with groups. This will tend to load the experience in the direction of failure for the worker and the group.

An example occurs when an agency uses group supervision of foster parents when such supervision was not previously part of the worker's function. The worker must learn the nature of the problems with which foster parents are concerned; at the same time he must learn how to supervise these parents and how to best use the group as a helping medium. The usual result of such ventures is that they evolve into either intensive psychotherapy sessions or superficial social gatherings aimed at improving the foster parents' identification with the agency. Most important, the potential for foster parents to come together to share and thus help each other on common problems is not realized. Learning a new method is best accomplished in relation to goals with which the worker has some knowledge, experience, and comfort.

PURPOSE

Categorical Group Services

Many agencies decide to have on-going group services for certain recurrent problems in their caseloads. Having established the group purpose, they then find people who are in need of the particular help. When this is done it is important to develop structures which are most prevalent in on-going casework function. In hospitals, social workers often help with the transitional states—orientation to the hospital, hospital adjustment, pre-discharge preparation, and post-discharge follow-up, accompanied by work with relatives in groups. The usual procedure calls for these groups becoming on-going and the individual's then being referred to or sought out for a group upon someone's identification of the appropriateness of that group service. Perhaps the most feasible prospect for psychiatric settings is that within this structure groups can be formed around more particularized needs and problems of the patients and relatives attending these groups. In any event, the example of pre-discharge preparation could represent the agency and worker purpose for forming the group. The particular goals of the individual members such as job finding and retirement could serve as indicators for grouping so that within the broad purpose of pre-discharge preparation the particular needs and interests of the members can be met.

II. GROUPING: SELECTING AND MATCHING GROUP MEMBERS

Two important questions that must be answered for each group are who and how many participants should be in the group. Beyond the factor of overall size the question of how many is closely related to the question of who. Generally, experience has indicated that for most social work treatment purposes, groups should be somewhere between five and twelve members and that eight is often optimum. Since most groups, particularly those with voluntary membership, have some degree of absences, it is desirable to have ten to twelve members in a group to insure that an average of eight or nine will attend any one meeting.

When dealing with groups of relatives, it is important to consider how many families are represented rather than just the total number of individuals involved. A minimum of five people should represent three or more families, since if only two families are represented competitive and/ or conflict situations might be stimulated. Similarly, if the group is to make decisions with any degree of frequency, it may be well to have an odd number of people in order to avoid tie votes.

The rationale for a five-to-twelve member group comes from many sources. Both experience and research indicate that if more than twelve members are present there is intensified subgrouping, and face-to-face interaction becomes more difficult. While the reasons for twelve may not be fully understood as yet, we do know that more than twelve members often results in a centralization of power which can subsequently result in one subgroup's leading and dominating the others. Actions will become chaneled through subgroup deliberation and thus make meetings more of a confrontation between subgroups rather than person-to-person relationships. An elaborate subgroup structure is beneficial for large decision-making groups like ward meetings, but it is not helpful for small treatment groups.

Similarity in Purpose

Similarities among the members should begin with the purpose of the group. If a group is formed as a result of identifying a common need among clients, grouping almost takes care of itself. The people for whom a common need or problem has been identified should obviously be placed in the same group. If, due to the exigencies of the agency, people having somewhat divergent purposes are grouped together, the worker must be prepared to spend part of the time serving one segment of the group and part of the time serving the other segments. During this time those members not concerned with a particular problem or need may become co-helpers of the worker and may intellectually deal with these problems or needs presented by the other subgroup. This will result in the treatment of one subgroup in front of and/or with the help of the other. When all the group members have similar strivings, then their involvement and help with other members will have more direct meaning to their own problem solutions.

The relative merits of group effort or individual effort can be debated, but experience has clearly demonstrated that grouping in accordance with the common, identifiable and meaningful purpose will result in (1) easier and quicker identification of the members with each other; (2) less difficulty in communication, expression, and exposure of self to each other; (3) harnessing the full power of the group for simultaneous help for its members; and (4) faster more identifiable problem-solving.

Two examples will serve to demonstrate these points:

A. A group of hospital patients was formed by a caseworker with the purpose of helping some male patients who were ready to move into the vocational rehabilitation program and prepare for ultimate discharge. These men, for various reasons, were all assessed by the ward team as ready to leave, but for many reasons were not responding to efforts aimed at helping them prepare for their discharge and jobs. The worker brought them together in a group and found that they were quickly able to identify their common problems, resistances, and strivings; to share some of their ideas, feelings, and difficulties; and to help each other move into the vocational rehabilitation programs preparing them for discharge. Eight of the ten members of this group left the hospital within six months after the group began. Most had become involved in a vocational rehabilitation effort and were either working or going on for more vocational help after leaving the hospital. The worker had the feeling that the group had done most of the work itself. She was being much too modest, since her sensitive help was a major factor. She was responding to the fact that she could spend most of her time helping the group to implement their goals and strivings without spending too much time reconciling conflicts over goals and focus. Communication among the members was strong from the time of the very first meeting. This in particular surprised the worker, since the members were all more reticent in larger and more diffuse ward meetings.

B. In a predischarge group for women, described in the previous section, the initial basis of commonality was found in the feelings of members about staying in or leaving the hospital. As the group progressed, the specifics of returning to their former situations or moving to a halfway house became more critical. At this point those who were returning to their former situations found much less benefit from discussions dealing with the halfway house, and vice versa. The worker had to alternate the focus between the two subgroups.

Many workers become concerned with homogeneity in a group when discussing similarities. The chances of having a homogenous group even when trying to establish one are remote. Homogeneity can be considered only in relation to particular characteristics. Group members may be somewhat homogeneous with regard to some characteristics, but there will be many others just as significant to make for heterogeneity. When we consider making a group homogeneous or at least similar with regard to the purposes of the members, we must think about all the member similarities or differences that we will have to take into account.

Differentials in Characteristics

Two categories of characteristics must be considered in grouping: 1) the motivation and capacity of members to use the group as a treatment medium, and 2) the motivation and capacity of the member to solve the common problem or to achieve the purpose with which the members are concerned.

Motivation and capacity to use a group. — There are many characteristics which have been suggested by various authors for use as criteria for grouping. With regard to motivation and capacity for use of the group as a treatment medium, a few rules of thumb can be useful. Some differences are desirable but combining of extremes is not. When there tends to be a wide disparity in either motivation or some capacities that have been bearing on the use of the group, an attempt should be made to have at least two members who share the difference rather than only one. Before getting into some examples, the worker must realize that there may be some group members who have little capacity to use the group situation for their own individual benefits. These people will need much help from the worker if they are to effectively participate with fellow members who have good capacity for use of the group.

The ability to communicate is one of the most important considerations for verbal treatment groups. Very often some withdrawn people will be placed in a group of very active speakers with the hope that this placement will get them talking more readily and effectively. Generally, the problem for the withdrawn person, however, is intensified by this rather than eased. It is only the unusual, withdrawn person who is able to begin more active communication through participation in such a group, and it is generally more useful to the withdrawn person to be placed in a group in which other people are similar to or are a little better in their capacity to communicate. Difficulty in communication can thus become one of the problems to which the group and the worker may direct their attention. Support with the resolution of the problem is potentially of greater benefit in this way than the sink or swim alternative which is often used.

At the other extreme, a very talkative member may dominate the meetings if there is no one else in the group who can enter into discussions as readily as he. Having at least two members who communicate easily will make it easier for all the others to join in. A whole group of overly talkative members will cause reduction in the talkativeness of each.

Lack of motivation for use of the group as a means for treatment need not contradict the use of group treatment however. What needs to be considered is the nature of any motivational lack or active resistance present. If poor motivation is due to actual or felt ineptness in inter-personal relations, some direct help on interpersonal relationships is in order. However, this help ought to be provided to a special group composed of people who have similar difficulties. Placement of persons with little or no motivation in a group in which most of the other members are well able to handle the interpersonal demands tends to increase the problem for the more inept member. A group of people with similar problems provides more opportunity for identification with and support of one another and this in turn will create more opportunity for direct problem solving.

If the motivational problem is due to a basic distrust of other people and projection as a defense is highly structured, a great deal of individual help should be provided for those involved before the group is considered as a treatment means. Such persons find the group too difficult a situation because there are too many people to watch, and all the energy is consumed in the watching. Milder and less structured forms of distrust and projective defenses can be lessened in a group through honest explorations of suspicions and acceptance by the other members and the worker. Projection is a defense that is least tolerated by other group members, and when it is used excessively the member will be subject to counterattack, which in turn will lead to either intensification of the projection or its removal as a defense.

A preponderance of self-oriented needs is often suggested as a contraindication for the use of group treatment. Here again, if an individual is preoccupied with himself and thrown into a group in which give and take are high among the other members, he may be rejected by them unless he changes quickly. A group of people with highly self-oriented needs will begin with a more primitive process but will grow in giving and getting at their own pace. This is another case in which preparation and learning from group participation will be necessary before the group can be used as a means for solution of other problems. In both cases of social ineptness and self-oriented needs a major part of the group purpose must become concerned with growth in group participation.

We could explore many other criteria for grouping, but all our efforts would not necessarily cover many of the considerations that would be important for the members of a particular group and a given agency. It is most important for the worker himself to consider the assets and liabilities demonstrated and incurred in past social

functioning of individual members. The next section will
further discuss the sources for such information.

Motivation and capacity to solve the common problem. — It has already been suggested that when the common problem is an inability to participate in groups, grouping on the basis of similarity is appropriate. When the common problem is based on the objectives beyond the immediate group, a diversity in the ways in which each member goes about solving the problem will be desirable. This very diversity may lend itself as a source from which the group derives its strength for problem-solving. Most groups would qualify since most people, even among hospitalized psychiatric patients, have sufficient capacity for treatment through participation. The exchange of different ideas about the same objective provides a firm basis for reciprocal influence and growth of all concerned. Therefore, a wide variety of feelings and opinions about the common problem is desirable. The underlying assumption is that a complementarity of strengths and limitations will be achieved among the members so that some members will help in the solution of problems in which they have particular mastery while receiving more help on other problems in which they tend to have more difficulty. The hope is that *each member will come out with different solutions from the other members* but that the new solutions will be more workable than the previous ones.

An example might be cited in the homemaker group for patients, discussed earlier. One woman was particularly adept at organizing her housework but had difficulty in "organizing her children." She felt resultant anger, which was a source of extreme distress for her. Another member "gave all" to her children and had

24

little energy left over for the management of her household. In the exchange of the group discussions the first patient learned something of the other's means for relating to her children, while the second patient learned something about becoming a little less involved with her children. The first patient learned to be a little more relaxed about her household and the second received some ideas about making her housework easier. Both explored the expectations of themselves as wives and mothers with more realistic appraisals resulting. Both became more comfortable with feelings of anger toward their children while a third group member influenced both of them in the direction of doing more for their own fulfillment.

An example of the effects of healthy diversity in motivation, for the purpose of the meeting, came in a group for husbands of hospitalized patients. In this group of seven husbands, two were quite positive about the value of the group and the need for change on their part to help in the recovery and rehabilitation of their wives. One member was strongly opposed to the group and wanted nothing to do with changing himself to better the relationship with his wife. The latter group member, who had been encouraged to share his feelings with the other group members, came to the first meeting on that basis. After a very heated argument the two "positively oriented" members had some healthy questioning about their involvement in the group, while the antagonistic member thought that there might be something to this after all. The particular issues for obtaining a good range of feelings and ideas will depend, of course, on the group, agency, and purpose of the meeting itself. While diversity in the ways of pursuing the goal may be desirable, extremes should be carefully considered. When extremes are used then it would be helpful to have at least two people sharing the extreme position.

III. INTAKE: FOUNDATION OF GROUP PARTICIPATION

There are three major objectives for the individual intake interview in any agency group service: 1) to help the client begin to consider his individual purposes and understand how they are similar to or different from the purposes of the agency and other group members; 2) to help the client prepare for using the group as a treatment medium; and 3) to initiate a worker-member relationship. Each of these objectives demands further commentary.

The number of intake interviews necessary will depend on the specific worker, group member, and group. In my own experience, one interview has usually been enough to accomplish intake for a group member. The danger in a series of individual intake interviews is that the client will begin to use the relationship to bring out material more appropriately saved for work within and through the group. Workers often find themselves continuing with a client on an individual basis as a result of prolonged pre-group individual contacts. Even in one interview, however, the client will try to use the worker

27

for individual treatment. This may be easily prevented by a worker maintaining a proper focus of the interview on preparation for group participation. When the client raises problems to which the group may be helpful, the worker should concentrate on interpreting to the client how he can best obtain help for his problem within the group. The success of the intake interview will depend on the worker's assurance that the group will be potentially effective. With this assurance, the worker will see less that needs to be done individually and more that can be accomplished within the group. Thus, as the worker gains more experience with treatment groups, he will be less vulnerable to the pratfalls of individual treatment from intake interviews.

Group Member's Purpose

If the group were established on the basis of common striving or problems identified in a given caseload, the worker and client must gain an understanding of how the prospective group member will view and feel about his problem. The worker must asses how this member's ideas and feelings about the common problems of all will agree with or differ from the ideas and feelings of other group members. Then the worker must help this prospective member to understand wherein his problem is similar to and wherein it is different from the problems of other group members. Even when the selection of members is on the basis of commonality, there usually will not be an exact similarity in their purposes for the group.

The worker's task thus far has been to help a given member consider or articulate his purpose and its relation to the purposes of the agency and of other group members. This process then paves the way for the group members to come together and through a process of deliberation establish a confluence of purposes, which in turn becomes the group purposes. The significance, attainment, and uses of this confluence will be discussed later in the chapter on "Starting the Group."

When the worker helps a client anticipate his commonalities of purpose with other group members, he accomplishes several goals: 1) he helps to reduce the individual member's anticipatory anxiety about the group; 2) he provides the member with a means for identification with other group members; 3) he facilitates communication from the outset of the group; and 4) he provides a basis for group formation and working on the common problems.

Preparing the new member for differences with other group members will help sustain him through the initial disagreements and conflicts he may face. While conflicts are not to be avoided in the group situation, their effects in the early stages could be harmful rather than beneficial. Conflict about significant issues is best reserved for a time when the group has established a means for resolving conflicts of a lesser nature. Early disagreements in the life of the group can lead to the elimination of some of its members, either by design of the rest of the group or by withdrawal of the individual member on his own accord.

INTAKE

Intake for Withdrawn Group

A sometimes articulate patient, who rarely expressed feelings, resented being placed in a withdrawn group. Most of the other members of this group expressed their feelings of fear or ineptitude in social contacts and thought that they would use the withdrawn group to overcome either or both. This particular member did not feel that he had any difficulty in talking but did suggest that he did not like small talk. He said that he enjoyed only deep intellectual conversations about important and enduring things, but thought matters of less consequence had little discussion value. During the course of the intake interview it became obvious to the worker that small talk among other things appeared to include expressions of feelings.

This client was able to consider using the withdrawn group to learn something about small talk and see if there was anything of value in it for him. He was advised by the worker that his purpose would be somewhat different from those of the other group members, but that, in the worker's opinion, it still was a valid use of this particular group. Entry into the group on this basis allowed this patient to participate actively and to be exposed to other views of problems inherent in communicating and relating to other people. While he achieved limited insight into his basic problem he did become better able to make small talk and to enjoy it. This let eventual expression of some of his feelings, particularly anger. In this case, the acceptance of the similarity in the communication problem was facilitated by allowing this client his view about how he was different. The difference appeared to help him accept participation in a group for a purpose which he could not otherwise accept.

Preparation for Group Experience

While striving toward the purpose of the group, a member is going to become involved in a group process. This group process will itself require something from each group member and will in turn give rise to supportive, corrective, and growth experiences for the member. People differ in their needs and desires to be group members. They also differ in capacities to participate in a given group. Very often in groups of people with emotional difficulty there are concomitant social difficulties. We must keep in mind that we are asking the group members to use the group situation to solve problems when group situations may not only be difficult for them but may also harbor some additional problems stemming from their own past experiences. It has already been suggested that when the additional problems become burdensome that some consideration should be given to having groups dealing directly with those problems that bear on group participation. As the worker gains more experience with particular types of groups he will find himself in an increasingly better position to evaluate difficulties and supports available for prospective group members. It would be most important to find out how the client feels toward the group as a medium of treatment and what his expectations are for himself and for other people in the group.

Past experiences with groups will certainly have their impact on a client's anticipation and use of the group.

Some may have had past treatment group experiences. Others may have had significant experiences in social clubs or school situations. Primary determinants might stem from early family experiences with particular emphasis on sibling relationships. Family experience should not be taken as fixed and unchangeable since the client may have had subsequent peer group relations which compensate for early familial difficulties. Most important for peer group determinants are the adolescent group experiences, since these are good barometers of capacity for group relationships.

Delving into past experience should be done by particularly focusing on implications for the treatment group participation. Certain misconceptions can be cleared up with simple explanations. Others may require a little more help in working through. Still more may be left for working out in the group situation itself.

A very common pre-set for entry into group treatment the first time is the classroom. This usually carries with it some notions about being told things (particularly what mistakes have been made) and intellectual learning. It also carries some connotations about the authority of the group worker and the subordinate role of the group member. Most clients can readily comprehend these differences with some help in sorting them out and after some demonstration. Real appreciation of the differences comes after the members have entered the group and feel the differences for themselves.

Intake for a Social Role Group

A female patient said that she did not like groups of women because they get very catty and cliquish. For this reason she did not want to participate in the group focused on preparation for leaving the hospital and again assuming the roles of wife and mother. While her particular reason was consistent with her diagnosis and personality dynamics, a realistic appraisal of this group, and other groups with her, resulted in her deciding to try it out in order to see for herself. Of particular importance was her notion that maybe the others had suffered similarly in such groups and might know better than to be catty or cliquish. The worker agreed with her and suggested that while other members may intend doing things differently some cattiness and cliquishness might still occur. A major difference would be that this group was concerned with correcting some of these problems so that the members would be working toward solution.

Establishing Relationship

The special nature of the worker-client(s) relationship is the most crucial aspect of group treatment. For this reason it has served as a basic point of conflict and misunderstanding between group workers and caseworkers for many years. The literature is replete with accusations that group workers are primarily concerned with their relationship to the group as a whole, while caseworkers are accused of relating only to individuals in the group. These accusations can only mean that the particular worker is overlooking his relationship to either individuals or the group as an entity. While seemingly an overwhelming task, the worker must constantly divide his attention between the group as an entity and its individual members. The worker must have a relationship with each group member, as well as with the group as a whole. To many without experience in work with groups, the dual focus appears an impossible task, and it may very well be if the worker holds himself responsible for knowing, observing, and intervening in all aspects of individual and group behavior. However, if the purpose of the group serves as a structure for organizing pertinent information about the individuals and the group as a whole, then a more selective and manageable basis of understanding in affect and behavior is possible. Both a dual focus and a dual relationship are facilitated by an individual intake interview.

After the group begins, the worker can use his relationship with the individual members as a bridge, if necessary, for members to relate to each other. The initiation of this relationship in an individual interview provides the basis for its use as a bridge to the other group members.

Without the individual interview, the worker will have to attempt to initiate relationships during the early group meetings. Initiation of individual relationships during group meetings will often result in an inordinately large amount of activity on the part of the worker. This early activity is carried out primarily to help the worker learn about the group, possibly to the exclusion of meeting the immediate needs of the members. Unfortunately, it might establish a pattern of dependence of the group on the worker. In other words, the need for the worker to have individual relationships with the group members is underscored, but *if an individual intake interview is used for this purpose then activity in the early group meetings can be devoted to facilitating member-to-member relationships instead of establishing worker-member relationships.*

The members may approach the group situation more easily when they have a relationship with the worker to fall back on, particularly if they find it difficult to establish relationships with the other group members themselves. The process of becoming a group will be discussed further in the chapter "Starting the Group". Suffice to say now that in most formed groups, members have no basis of past experience with each other and have not as yet developed a means of communication, ways of relating to each other, or affectional ties. They are simply a collection of people who happen to be in the same place at the same time. If the worker at this time has to establish individual relationships, then his efforts may be at the expense of promoting communication among the members themselves.

The most difficult part of the worker-client(s) relationship for workers whose past experience has been mainly one-to-one relationship is sharing the helping function with the group members. Promoting member-to-member help is closely akin to the support and enhancements of self-dependent action with the individual client. More of the worker's direct efforts in group work thus become concerned with enabling or facilitating this member-to-member self-help and less of his efforts are directed towards helping the individual member. A problem solution not within the capacity of one client may be within the ego capacity of other group members. As a result, the worker should be attempting to help those with the better ego capacity in the particular problem area to assist in the problem-solving process. However, there are many instances in which the worker's direct assistance to individuals will be essential. The problem of the worker's role vis-a-vis the group members' role in helping is less difficult when dealing with purposefully formed groups. *When a co-problemed member helps somebody in the group with a similar problem, he is also working toward a resolution of his own difficulties.* When a worker is involved in helping the individual member either directly or by facilitating the help of other members for the individual, he is active as a professional helper and not a co-problemed member.

It would be appropriate at this point to consider the position of the worker with respect to the group. Many workers confuse the worker's position as a group leader with an indigenous leader of the group. An indigenous leader is a group member who, because of certain qualities or capacities, assumes or is assigned a position of influence over his fellow members in the group. The worker with the group attains his position of leadership by virtue of his representing the agency, being designated as the professional helper to the group, and because of his expertise. Even if the worker wanted to divest himself of this authority derived from the agency and professional expertise, he could not. As a result, the professional worker does not become one of the group members even though at times the worker may offer direct suggestions "as if" he were one of the group members.

If the worker develops some vested interest as a member of the group, he is often open for a group facsimile of countertransference. When some of the group members have a disagreement or conflict, the worker's role should be that of lending *support to both sides* is helping them find means for negotiating their individual differences. If the worker has vested interest in one point of view this should either be weeded out of the worker's assistance or at least expressed as a definite and personal opinion. What should be avoided at all costs is the worker's joining one part of a group in helping to win an argument over another part of the group. The role of arbitrator cannot be assumed by the worker if he is cast in the role of a group member. Since helping groups to resolve conflicts is one of the most **critical** functions of a worker with a group, careful **consideration** must be given to the establishment of the worker-client(s) relationship in which the worker does not **become a** fellow group member.

IV. STARTING THE GROUP: HELPING THE GROUP TO FORM

A major objective for the first group meeting is to help the group begin to develop and work on the group purpose. This requires an integration of individual and agency purposes which in turn become the group purposes. It also requires the group members to get to know each other, begin to communicate with each other, and begin to help each other toward their common goals.

A first step in any beginning group is the introduction of members to each other. This can be accomplished before the meeting begins while everyone is in the room or as the first item of discussion. Name tags, particularly in larger groups, can be very helpful in the getting-to-know-you process.

While it begins with introductions, the process of getting to know each other will indirectly or directly continue throughout the first few meetings. For this reason, the next step is for the worker to introduce discussion of the commonalities of purpose that brought the group together. A discussion of these commonalities at

41

the outset will help toward effecting a confluence of agency and member goals into group goals, building on the preparation in the intake interview, and providing a focus with which all members can work.

The members will attempt to answer some or all of the following questions from the outset:

1. Who is here?
2. Why are they here?
3. Where do I fit in?
4. How do I compare with others?

While the process of finding out about each other will go on indefinitely, the stress on what each has in common with the others will help all the members to feel that the others are in the same boat and that they are reasonably similar on matters of consequence.

The initial discussion of purpose may take many forms. Some groups will tangle with it directly through sharing their ideas for the group and even what they expect from the leader and from each other. Sometimes, if the group has too many members with severe relationship problems, a purpose discussion will be difficult. Most often though an initial discussion of purpose will be similar to the following example, which represents a typical way in which group members come to grips with the questions of purpose and getting to know each other at the initial meeting.

The Start of a Parent's Group

Each of the group members of one group had a young adult son or daughter in a psychiatric hospital. The worker introduced the members to each other as they gathered in the meeting room. Since, from intake, they knew that everyone else had a son or daughter on the same unit, members were informally trying to match the parents with the patients. The worker then started the meeting with an affirmation of the fact that they were all facing similar and difficult situations in having a son or daughter hospitalized because of a psychiatric problem. The worker further emphasized that, while each situation was unique, there were many similarities in what parents were facing. For this reason the hospital staff thought that bringing them together would give them an opportunity for some help from the hospital as well as from each other on this difficult situation.

One mother then suggested that each tell a little bit about his son's or daughter's problem so that they would all have more understanding when discussing any particular problems raised. Everyone readily agreed and they spent a good part of the meeting listening to each couple express their particular concerns. Some questions for further information were asked and comments were made on the similarities among the problems for and with the patients.

This group's way of discussing its similarities in purpose was to hear the more pertinent details about the patients involved and from this determine what particular similarities and differences were important to them all as a group. Groups composed of the spouses of patients may be a little more general in their initial discussion however, because they often feel that more risk of themselves is involved. Some patient groups will be too highly specific and elaborate in the first meeting and so venture farther than the members are ready to go. If discussion is not limited it can result in some members not returning out of sheer embarrassment or fear of exposing too much of themselves too soon. In contrast, a more diverse group, such as combinations of parents of patients and spouses of patients, will spend an inordinately large amount of time trying to prevent meaningful discussion in direct and tangential attempts to establish a satisfactory common purpose.

Most hospital groups will try to begin with questions directed to the staff. These questions will be about the hospital, treatment, mental illness, or the reason for the group. Some of these questions should be answered directly, particularly when they require knowledge expected of a staff member. Leading the group around to the right answer that the worker has already in mind is inadvisable and potentially harmful to the group's development.

If the group members have much in common, then many initial questions can be turned back to the group for discussion. Most of these questions will have some significant meaning for all the members. When the members of a group have less in common with each other, however, it will be more difficult to turn questions back to the group and most of the worker's answers will have meaning only for particular individuals. Answers by other members in a diverse group will usually be given in an intellectualized way since there is little chance that their answers have resulted from personal experience and concern. In a group with common purpose, the discussion and answers will be based on similar, meaningful experiences, and the complementarity of members' knowledge and experiences will allow them to help each other.

Many of these problems did not arise in the parent's group mentioned above because of pre-group planning and preparation. By the time all the members got to the group they needed only a reminder from the worker about their purpose in the group and with one additional suggestion by a member concerning procedure they launched into an active and meaningful discussion.

Workers often ask how active or inactive they should be at first or how they should start the group meeting. If the purpose is clear, a discussion of purpose should be able to facilitate the beginning more quickly. If there is difficulty in starting with the purpose, then that difficulty should be explored immediately. Initial problems may usually be traced to oversights in planning and preparation of the group and its members, particularly with respect to individual and agency purposes.

A typical example of a starting problem occurred in one group organized for the spouses and parents of patients. The first four meetings consisted of questions and answers, or questions and no answers. Questions were concerned with hospital rules, medication, treatment program in the hospital, the patients, and gripes concerning all of these. When a particular question was answered, then the particular discussion ended and either silence or another unrelated question ensued. If there were no answers to the question forthcoming, then a degree of hostility pervaded the meeting—much of that hostility directed toward the worker. Faltering attempts to establish some helpful discussion on commonalities resulted in short-lived conflicts which became repressed.

Spouses felt that the parents might have had some difficulties too but that these did not help *them* to understand *their* situation. The reverse was true for the parents. Discussion became superficial with little risk involved and the only subjects on which a few sustained discussion took place were those pertaining to the life and progress of patients in the hospital and how relatives might approach those patients. Unfortunately, there was only a limited discussion of pre- and post-hospital relationships. If the purpose of the group had been psychotherapy there may have been many useful instances of transferences among the members taking place with parents representing parents or in-laws and spouses representing children. The same conflicts inhibiting the ego-supportive approach could have been used as material for group psychotherapy. In this way the diverse group could either function on a superficial or deep psychtherapeutic basis but not on a significant reality basis with the pertinent facts and feelings surrounding the problem at hand.

V. SOME GROUP TREATMENT TECHNIQUES: HELPING IN THE WORK OF THE GROUP

Those group treatment techniques discussed here are closely akin to ego-supportive casework techniques. They are not exactly the same, of course, since the complicating factor of the group requires special adaptations in the thinking and actions of the worker. Knowledge of a few factors about groups and group processes may be particularly important for caseworkers before they consider techniques.

First of all the worker must remember that a group is always composed of individual members. At times the members will be working in harmony toward common objectives but at other times they will be in conflict and even in complete disorganization. The organization of any group for the development and implementation of its goals is called the process of group formation. The result of group formation is a structure by which the group co-ordinates and directs its efforts toward achieving its goals.

Most groups move through many states and levels of

formation and disorganization during their life spans. It is important to keep this firmly in mind so that what one member says is not attributed to the group as a whole. *The expression of one person may or may not be representative of the ideas or feelings of the rest of the members.*

The task of the worker is always to help the group to form and to achieve its goals by the best means possible. Each goal may require some reformation of the group for its attainment, but it will never be as difficult after the first goal achievement. For the treatment group, the process of formation and goal achievement requires a few fundamental steps. While these phases may go on simultaneously the following set of questions which the group strives to answer may be helpful in identifying the phases:

1. What are we going to do?
2. How are we going to do it?
3. Who will be the one(s) to do it?
4. Will we be able to do it?

If the group was not formed on the basis of common strivings, then the first question becomes crucial. Sufficient time should be spent in considering and clarifying the group purpose and in formulating some group goals. Because of overt and covert demands which members bring to the group, there must be some assurance that each individual will have an impact on the group's goals and as a result some stake in the outcome. Any conflicts will manifest themselves either in direct discussion of purpose or in individual attempts to raise conflicting or mutually exclusive questions and problems for the group to solve. When the grouping has been done with commonality of purpose in mind, the determination of the goals will be relatively easy.

The discussion and clarification of how the work will be done will be a matter of interpretation, i.e. how other groups have done this in the past, demonstration in the early stages of the group, relevant past experiences of members. The members must be involved in offering their own ideas from the very beginning particularly in relation to the how of the work.

Who will do it encompasses the worker and the group members. Most groups in the early stages will want the worker to do most of the work. A major part of the problem will come when the members, faced with their past failures to cope with problems and other people, feel overwhelmed by the prospect of trying to cope with their problems in a situation involving other people. If there are similarities among the members and common strivings then these become a source of reinforcement of both the strength and hope of the members. Common strivings for group members function similar to individual modification. A group with unclear, diffuse, or dissimilar strivings is akin to an unmotivated or ambivalent individual client. An extremely diverse treatment group becomes a collection of individuals for which the worker is the focal point of communication and action.

Facilitating Communication and Participation

Verbal communication requires both a sender and a receiver. Someone must do the talking and someone must listen, understand, and sympathize for the act of communication to be completed. *The foremost job of the worker with a group is to facilitate communication among the members of that group.* The worker's attention must be given to aiding members to talk and while doing so make themselves understood by the other members of the group. Also the worker must help other members understand the member speaking. It is not enough for the worker himself to understand and sympathize with what a member is trying to communicate.

If he is to become a group participant, each member must be able to communicate with the other members. Otherwise, all communication will become channeled through the worker. If a member says something to which others respond and the sender seems satisfied then the communication is complete. If the member has difficulty in expressing his thoughts and feelings, the worker should help him or help other members to help him. To do so may require helping the individual to feel more at ease, sympathizing with him in the difficulty inherent in the subject, or assisting him in expressing the desired message or feeling from an unintelligible jumble of words. It may require asking a member exactly what he has said. If the other members do not seem to fully understand, it is important to engage them in the process of trying to clarify the meaning for themselves. If they do understand but do not respond, the worker may then need to recall attention to the communication. Particularly in the early stages of the group, a first communication effort will have significant bearing on subsequent communication, both from the individual and from the other group members who may be watching what is happening. A worker's calling attention to any overlooked communication lends support to that communication and gives at least a sign of the worker's interest at the same time it shows the member that what he has to say may be valued by the worker and possibly by the other group members.

Quiet group members should generally be allowed to watch and enter in as they feel ready. If a member continues to come and remains silent, the chances are that he is getting something from the group. However, the worker should look for the non-verbal signs of interest and readiness since a question or invitation to comment *at the right moment* can help the silent member over the difficulty of starting to talk. During intake, the worker should have found some clues to concerns and interests of each member. The directed questions or invitations should deal with a subject on which the silent member feels most comfortable. Sometimes the worker can introduce a subject which will offer an opening for the silent member to take.

Group silences generally create no problem in small, purposefully formed groups. Silence itself is a form of communication. However, the meaning of the silence can at best only be a matter of speculation unless, of course, the members discuss the reason for the silence. Silence can mean that the members are too angry to talk; it can mean that they are not sure where to go from where they are; or it can mean simply that they do not have anything further to say. Instead of playing the waiting game to see whose anxiety will push someone to talk first, it is best for the worker to comment on the fact that the group is silent. If nothing happens, a question pertaining to the silence will usually produce results. Silence should not be overlooked by the worker, but it should not be allowed to continue for more than a few minutes unless it is part of what the group consciously intends to do at the time.

Dealing directly with the silence, as indicated above, will usually bring about one of two results. One is that a discussion of the nature and causes of the silence will ensue. This discussion might also entail working through resistances to talking at the time. A second possibility is that one of the members will try to initiate a discussion of some concern. If the rest of the members respond and begin to discuss this concern, it is usually wise to allow the discussion to proceed, unless, of course, what the individual introduces seems clearly to be done only to throw the group off its perscribed course or to conceal the real issues at hand. If there is great difficulty in talking, it may be well to go back to probing the silence or reluctance to speak.

Resolving Conflict and Decision-making

Varied opinions are the life blood of any group if that group is to be a vehicle for growth and help for its members. The conflicts with which we are concerned include a wide range—from the broad purpose of the group, through what should be discussed next, to differing opinions about the problem at hand and its solution. Any conflicts that result will be caused by differences of opinions and feelings of the members about the subject and about each other as well as by the pattern of relationships of each of the members before its initial development and while in the group. The worker should not lose sight of the fact that without conflict the group will be valueless to its members, since there will be no means for change to result.

Some conflicts will need to be resolved while others will be best allowed to go unresolved. Conflict about what to discuss has to be resolved, for no discussion can take place until it is. If the conflict is about how to solve a particular common problem, each member should come up with his own unique solution. The worker will have to assess whether his job is to help the group deliberate and thus resolve the disagreement or whether he has to help the members allow differences of opinion to exist.

The methods for helping in the resolution of conflict are based on early detection and taking manageable portions or issues for the group to consider. Successful experience with manageable portions or issues usually results in an increased capacity of the group to resolve larger or more complex conflicts. As has been mentioned earlier under intake and relationship, the worker should give his opinion directly to the group or keep his own opinion under disciplined management, without allowing it to support one side of the group in conflict against the other side.

The best evidence that the worker is in a neutral position will come from his seeing some significant value to both sides of any question. Then the worker can lend support to the expression of both sides of the issue. It is important for the worker to make sure that each side understands the other. If there are many aspects to the issue or multiple issues, it is helpful for the worker to pull out one manageable piece for a starter and limit deliberation to that.

For example, a member of a pre-discharge group did not want to discuss the topic of job interviews because he thought the member who proposed the subject usually talked too much about it and did not give others a chance to participate. The worker separated the issues and limited discussion to the issue of the job interview, suggesting that if the topic were chosen, then they could discuss the other member's domination of the discussion. This led to quick acceptance of the topic as pertinent to all concerned and then to a discussion of the member's dominance of discussions. The dominating member was thus able to accept some limitation on his participation by the other group members and both sides received something in the resolution of these two issues. The worker's separation of the issues and support for both sides of each issue, facilitated the resolution.

More often the conflicts are more covert. During the discussion of one subject a member may begin to talk about something else. It may be a reaction to the subject under discussion or it may be an attempt to provoke the group or the worker. Of course there are a host of other possibilities. But despite the reason for the shift, it is this member's vote for something else and should be considered as such. To place a limit on interruptions may mean keeping the members from dealing with their reaction to the subject under discussion or with their relationship to each other. The reaction may be pursued at the expense of something in which the rest of the group wishes to work. Sometimes the worker will need to make a decision for the group, but whenever possible it is more helpful for the worker to bring the alternatives into focus for the group. Even if the motivation for the interruption is based on some essential need to test or be provocative, focusing on the conflict with lead to helping each member work out some of the difficulties with the other member. It may also happen that most of the other members would also like to change the focus for discussion at the time.

Confrontation with Interpersonal Behavior

Confrontation of the group with their behavior is akin to confrontation of the individual with his behavior in a one-to-one relationship. However, confrontation in a group can have a far-reaching impact on the members even without the use of depth insight into individual personalities.

When two or more people in a group are behaving in certain ways toward each other, it is usually easier for them and everyone else to be aware of this, particularly after it is pointed out by the worker or after it is pointed out by another group member. Moreover, pointing out interpersonal behavior patterns in a group has a similar effect to making an interpretation, in that, once seen and accepted, that particular mode of behavior may be modified. When a defense is interpreted to an individual it will usually result in discomfort with or discontinuance of its use in the given situation. Unless it is replaced by something else it will undoubtedly come out in other ways.

Similarly, in the group situation a pattern of behavior once pointed out needs to be explored for its meaning and feeling for all concerned. Alternative modes of behavior must be forthcoming if the behavior is to change and the needs underlying the behavior acceptably met. Change in a group treatment situation gains support from the better acceptance of the individual by the other members, plus the experience of using the new way in the actual social situation of the treatment group. It is important to emphasize that the worker not identify with one person's behavior pattern over another since the behavior of the two in their interpersonal relationship will usually be reciprocal and serve the needs of each.

For example, one group member's domination of the meeting can be possible only if the other members allow it. If others wish to dominate, a conflict will result. If one member dominates and the others submit, there is no conflict. When the worker points out that one member is dominating and the others are submitting to this domination, he will create an uneasiness with the existing pattern on both sides. If he sides with the submissive members, the worker is discounting the possible reticence, fear, or anxiety that these members have about becoming active. If the worker assumes that both sides contribute to creating the dominant-submissive pattern, he can take a supportive approach to both and even enlist the entire group to help itself be less extreme, if this is the objective.

VI. TERMINATION: BRIDGE TO SELF DEPENDENCE

Purposeful formation of a group can simplify the termination process. If a purpose was based on common problems or needs, a point will come when the members begin to feel that they have gone as far as they can in this group, in the mastery of their problem, or in meeting the individual needs or goals. Just as in work with individuals, the detection and raising of this culmination may begin either with the worker or with the clients. The decision to terminate should of course be a joint worker-group decision. Depending on the nature of the group and the nature of the purpose, plans can be made for either a rapid or a tapering type of termination.

If the group is open-ended (meaning that members enter and leave the group at different times), more emphasis must be placed on the individual attainment of the desired goals. When the group is closed (meaning that members all start together and finish together), the state of the whole group must be considered and evaluated.

A pre-discharge group most often ends for a member when he is discharged. However, some pre-discharge groups terminate members when they are actively working with vocational rehabilitation and-or other services. Other pre-discharge groups allow members to come back after they leave the hospital. Generally, the clearer the purpose, the more obvious will be the point of termination for members and the worker. In one group for orienting patients to a hospital, it was unusual to find a patient who wanted to continue after the third group meeting. In an open post-discharge group, most members began to miss meetings after their first six months. These members were supported in their tapering off in attendance.

When an individual member terminates with a group, problems are created for both the member and the rest of the group. As in any case of separation, if the group has been a satisfying experience, the members will feel some loss with concomitant anger, but will be able to handle the separation more adequately.

For the rest of the group, there is the problem of replacing the individual's role and function in the group. If this were a leadership function, there might be a need for major reforming or there might be a temporary gap. Even if there were a ready replacement from within or without the group, the group will never be exactly the same again. Usually, never being the same needs to be examined fully with the remaining members since they may consciously or unconsciously expect the group to remain the same. They may not be satisfied with the new form of the group until they can accept the fact that each group *must* be different in some ways from all other groups.

The anger aroused by the separation is often difficult for members to express since they usually feel that it is unjustified to feel angry about this. As a result, efforts to help the members to express anger over a separation may not meet with immediate success. Instead a period of depression ensues in which the group occupies itself with tangential material or indirect expression of anger. There may, for example, be some morbid discussion around seemingly unrelated matters. With or without direct help from the worker, this depression will usually be followed by renewed vigor on the part of the group. Direct expression of angry feelings about the separation may or may not be part of this renewed activity. This will depend on the ability of the group to express itself on any matter.

In groups where everyone is terminating, the depression will often be followed by phases of group and/or individual regression as well as periods in which the group and/or members become overly self-sufficient. It is important for the worker during these periods to recognize the regression and not allow it to push him into *taking over* again for the group and its members since this will further the regression and undercut the potential self-dependence of the members after leaving the group. It is equally important for the worker not to feel rejected by the group when they shut him out and demonstrate their self-dependence. The danger for the worker here is in possible efforts to make the group *need* him again. In both instances, the important function for the worker is to help the group to maintain its achieved level of function and realistically prepare for the termination. Two kinds of foci for group discussion will be helpful to the group in preparing for termination. First is a discussion of the process by which the members achieved the level of interacting and problem-solving which made it possible to consider termination. This discussion might also include gains that the members have made during the course of the treatment process and might also include comparing where they are at the end with where they were at the start. Second is a discussion of how the members are realistically handling problems outside the group which initially brought them into the treatment process. Good signs of ability to handle these initial problems are the members' readiness and ability to cope with them as well as their readiness and ability to seek further help in the future if their coping efforts don't work out.

In groups where some are terminating and others continuing, the separation process will culminate in renewed strivings toward the goal of the group. There may be need for rediscussion of the what, how, and who will do the work, and depending on the function of the member who left, there may also be some need to again discuss their feelings about ability to do the work. The process just described constitutes a major reformation of the group. The result of this process should be a new group which will probably be somewhat different than previously but ready for work again.

The affectional ties that developed in the group's life may be difficult for members to relinquish. Many members of treatment groups comment that this is the first time that they ever had such close and satisfying relationships. Much support needs to be given in such instances; for once having made friends, group members have better chances for doing so again. This is very difficult for them to accept, but it does happen.

In both the purpose and the interpersonal dimensions of the group, efforts should be made to help the members become aware of other resources that may continue to help or be available in case they need them. As it is very unlikely that they will ever have this same group available for help again, preparation for this fact is essential. It is important for the members to consider that, while the new group may be different, some of the same basic elements utilized to help them will again be available to them.

Similarly, on the personal relationship side, the members should be helped through direct discussion in the group on how they can carry over to their outside social life that which they have learned about relating to others in the treatment group. If that outside situation was too constricted, referral to resources for social contact in the community should be made in order to help the members capitalize and maximize on what has been gained.

Finally, many groups make plans to continue on, either on a helpful or friendly basis, after leaving the agency. Unless there is some potential for mutually destructive behavior, there is no reason to discourage this trend toward the continuance of friendships. However, despite many plans and hopes, very few group members do continue contacts very far beyond the end of group treatment. Apparently, when a member joins a group for a meaningful purpose in common with the other members, the need for the group and the other members within it decreases after that purpose has been reasonably fulfilled.

VII. SUMMARY

Realistically, the worker must realize that no specific suggestions for the establishment of purpose can be set down since they must result from the policy and specific exigencies of individual agencies. However, the worker should recognize that the purpose of the group should fall within the usual function of the agency-worker with clients. That purpose should have significant meaning for all the individual members of the group. A common identifiable purpose should help the group to form and the members to become engaged in a mutual sharing and solving of their common problems.

When a predetermined purpose is imposed, then it is important to reconcile and subdivide the members selected in accordance to their particular commonalities with respect to agency goals. To the degree that there are divergencies in purpose there will be the necessity for accommodation and compromise in the focus of the meeting. Extreme divergence is likely to lead to individual treatment in front of other people, to increase the tendency

64

toward inordinate transference development, to increase the dependency of the group on the worker, and finally to run the risk of ego weakening. It will also make participation by members more difficult and will require the worker to divert his efforts from goal production or problem solving, to helping the group to form, communicate, and maintain itself as an organization.

Once the worker has realized this, then he must not forget that the most desired grouping method will be concerned with those people in a caseload among whom a common need, problem, or striving is detected. Most useful for *this* purpose is the practice of beginning with the identification of common problems in the existing, or waiting list, caseload of the agency. When a predetermined purpose or structure is imposed, a group should then be homogeneous with regard to the purpose which individual members and the agency identify for the group. Some difference with regard to the motivation and capacity of the members to use the group experience can be allowed but careful attention should be given to avoiding extremes. When one extreme is included then it is advisable to have two or more people who share the extreme of the characteristic. A range of differences in motivations and capacities to achieve the purpose of the group is desirable. The development of a complementarity in strengths and limitations is of utmost importance for promoting variety and growth in coping efforts. With the many possible criteria for grouping and the subsequent impracticability or impossibility of considering all of them for productive grouping, the worker must concern himself mainly with those characteristics that have significant bearing on the member's use of the group and his pursuit of the group goals in problem-solving efforts.

The next concern for the worker revolves around an individual intake interview which should be used for initiating a worker-client relationship while preparing the client for the group experience, and to make use of the group for solving his problems. Intake helps the worker maintain a dual focus on the group and individual members at one and the same time. The development of group purpose should be aided by means of the pre-group exploration of individual purposes with each member.

Once this exploration has taken place, the worker can help the group begin from the groundwork in the planning and preparation. If a group begins for a common purpose which is meaningful to its members, and if the members are prepared for participation in the group to attain the common purpose, then starting almost takes care of itself. The members will find it easier to communicate, to identify, to risk, to help, and perhaps most important of all, to be helped. A worker with such a group will find it less necessary to stimulate or provoke discussion and will be able to devote more effort in helping the group and individuals move toward common goals. This common purpose will also free the worker to assist individual members with difficulties in group participation, in their goal strivings, and aid all of the members to help each other.

Once the group has formed around some purposes which are clear and held in common by the members, the worker can direct his efforts toward facilitating the problem solving work. Three major ways in which a worker can assist the group in solving its common problems are: first, to help the members communicate and interact. Next, once the members are interacting, the worker can help the group to facilitate the resolve of disagreements, conflicts, and antagonisms. Third, the worker can help the group to facilitate the modification of maladaptive patterns of behavior through confrontation and working through the problematic behavior.

When a group is established with harmony in agency-worker, individual, and group purpose, then the probability is increased that the experience will be successful for all concerned. Harmony of purposes and successful experience will facilitate the termination process. If the treatment and termination processes contain direct assistance in the transfer of learning from the group situation to the actual life situations of the members, then there is more likelihood that the end of the group leads to increased mastery and self-dependence in the members' life adjustments.

TOPICAL BIBLIOGRAPHY

Books and articles appearing in this bibliography are not necessarily endorsed by the author. They are provided so that readers can have exposure to a variety of opinions on the subject and be freer to develop their own notions about work with groups. Those articles or books marked with an asterisk, however, are highly recommended by the author for both their value in ideas and their basic necessity for undergirding practice.

FEELINGS OF THE WORKER AT THE START

* Williams, Meyer, Ph.D., "Limitations, Fantasies, and Security Operations of Beginning Group Psychotherapists." *The International Journal of Group Psychotherapy.* XVI (April 1966), pp. 150-162. This article is a must for anyone who formerly did only individual treatment and is contemplating the start of a group.

FEELINGS OF THE MEMBERS AT THE START

Konopka, Gisela, "Resistances and Hostility in Group Members." *Group Work Foundations and Frontiers,* Harleigh Trecker, ed. New York, Whiteside, Inc. and William Morrow and Co. (1955), pp. 130-142.

PURPOSES FOR GROUPS

* Phillips, Helen, "Group Services to Clients: Purposes and Process." *Child Welfare,* XLII, No. 6 (June 1963), pp. 265-72. Operation of purposes from the group worker's points of view.

Cartwright, Dorwin, and Zander, Alvin, *Group Dynamics.* Evanston, Ill., Row Peterson, Second Edition (1960), pp. 395-486. Operation of purposes from the social psychology point of view.

Klein, Joyce Gale, "Adult Education and Treatment Groups in Social Agencies" (a dissertation), Washington, D. C., The Catholic University of America Press, (1960). A study of the purposes for which groups are employed in a range of casework settings.

THE DYNAMICS OF GROUPS FROM A
SOCIAL PSYCHOLOGICAL VIEWPOINT

Cartwright, Dorwin, and Zander, Alvin, *Group Dynamics.* Evanston, Ill., Row Peterson, Second Edition (1960), pp. 395-486.

Homans, George C., *The Human Group.* New York, Harcourt Brace, (1950).

Olmsted, Michael S. *The Small Group.* New York, Random House, (1959).

Sprott, W. J. H. *Human Groups.* Baltimore, Penguin Books, (1958).

Thelin, Herbert, *Dynamics of Groups at Work.* Chicago, University of Chicago Press, (1954).

THE DYNAMICS OF GROUPS FROM A PSYCHOANALYTIC VIEWPOINT

Scheidlinger, Saul, *Psychoanalysis and Group Behavior: A Study of Freudian Group Psychology.* New York, Norton, (1952).

Slavson, S. R., "Analytic Group Psychotherapy." New York, Columbia University Press, (1950).

TOPICAL BIBLIOGRAPHY

THE DYNAMICS OF GROUPS FROM A TREATMENT ORIENTATION

* Bernstein, Saul, "Conflict and Group Work." *Explorations in Group Work.* Boston University School of Social Work, (1965).

* Garland, James A., Jones, Hubert E., and Kolodny, Ralph L., "A Model for Stages of Development in Social Work Groups." *Explorations in Group Work.* Boston, Boston University School of Social Work, (1965).

TOPICAL BIBLIOGRAPHY

THE RELATIONSHIP BETWEEN GROUPWORK, GROUP TREATMENT, AND CASEWORK

Bartlett, Harriet M., "The Generic - Specific Concept in Social Work Education and Practice." *Issues in American Social Work,* A. J. Kahn, ed. New York, Columbia University Press, 1959.

Burns, Mary and Glasser, Paul, "Similarities and Differences in Casework and Groupwork Practice." *Social Service Review,* XXXVIII (December, 1963), pp. 416-28.

Falck, Hans, "The Use of Groups in the Practice of social Work." *Social Casework,* XLIII, No. 7 (July, 1962), pp. 347-54.

Fisher, Raymond, "Use of Groups in Social Treatment by Caseworkers and Group Workers," in Use of Groups in the Psychiatric Setting. New York, National Association of Social Workers, (1958), pp. 23-33.

Kendall, Katherine A., "New Dimensions in Casework and Group Work Practice: Implications for Professional Education." *Social Work,* Vol. IV, October, 1959, pp. 49-56.

Klein, Joyce Gale, "Social Group Treatment: Some Selected Dynamics." *New Perspectives on Services to Groups.* New York, National Association of Social Workers, (1961), pp. 35-47.

* Schwartz, William, "The Social Worker in the Group," in *New Perspectives on Services to Groups,* New York, National Association of Social Workers (1961), pp. 7-34.

Sherman, Sanford, "The Choice of Group Therapy for Casework Clients." *Social Work Practice Selected Papers: National Conference on Social Welfare, 1962.* New York, Columbia University Press, (1962), pp. 174-86.

BASIC REFERENCES ON SOCIAL GROUP WORK

* Bernstein, Saul, ed., *Explorations in Group Work*. Boston, Boston University School of Social Work (1965).

Coyle, Grace L., *Group Experience and Democratic Values*. New York, The Woman's Press, 1947.

Coyle, Grace L., *Group Work with American Youth*. New York, Harper, 1948.

* Konopka, Gisela, *Social Group Work: A Helping Process*. Englewood Cliffe, New Jersey, Prentice-Hall, 1963.

* Phillips, Helen U., *Essentials of Group Work Skill*. New York, Association Press, 1957.

Schwartz, William, "The Social Worker in the Group." *The Social Welfare Forum,* National Conference on Social Welfare, (1961), pp. 146-77.

Vinter, Robert D., "Group Work: Perspectives and Prospects." *Social Work With Groups,* National Association of Social Workers, (1959), pp. 128-48.

Vinter, Robert D., "Social Group Work." *Encyclopedia of Social Work.* New York, National Association of Social Workers, (1965), pp. 715-24.

Wilson, Gertrude, and Ryland, Gladys, *Social Group work Practice.* Massachusetts, The Riverside Press, 1949.

BASIC REFERENCES ON GROUP PSYCHOTHERAPY

Rosenbaum, Max and Berger, Milton, *Group Psycho-therapy and Group Function.* New York, Basic Books, Inc., 1963.

Whitaker, Dorothy Stock, and Lieberman, Morton A., *Psychotherapy Through the Group Process.* New York, Atherton Press, 1964.

TREATMENT TECHNIQUES IN SOCIAL WORK WITH GROUPS

Direct discussion of treatment techniques per se is rather limited in group treatment literature. Techniques generally must be gleaned from expressed or implied suggestions in much of the literature. The following are a few direct attempts to discuss techniques specifically.

Churchill, Sallie, "Prestructuring Group Content." *Social Work,* IV, No. 3 (July 1959), pp. 52-59.

* Bernstein, Saul, ed., *Explorations in Group Work.,* Boston, Boston University School of Social Work, 1965.

* Frey, Louise A., "Support and the Group: Generic Treatment Form." *Social Work,* IXVII, No. 4, (October, 1962), pp. 35-42.

EXPERIENCES WITH GROUPS AND APPLICATIONS OF GROUP METHODS

Ackerly, Ethel Grumman and Flegel, Beverly R., "A Social Work Approach to Street Corner Girls." *Social Work,* V October, 1960, pp. 27-36.

Albee, Constance Impallaria, "Group Work with Hospitalized Children." *Children* II, No. 6 (November-December, 1955), pp. 217-21.

Auerbach, Aline B., "Parent Group Education and Leadership Training." *Child Study Association.* New York, 1957.

Austin, David N., "Goals for Gang Workers." *Social Work,* II (October, 1957), pp. 43-50.

Barnes, Marion, Schiff, Edward, and Albee, Constance, "The Collaboration of Child Psychiatry, Casework and Group Work in Dealing with the Mechanism of Acting Out." *The American Journal of Orthopsychiatry,* XXVII (April, 1957), pp. 377-86.

Bell, Courtenay, and Kaplan, Harvey, "Public-Voluntary Sponsorship of a Mothers' Group." *Social Casework,* XLV, No. 1(January, 1964), pp. 21-25.

Blum, Arthur, "Peer-Group Structure and a Child's Verbal Accessibility in a Treatment Institution." *Social Service Review,* XXXVI, No. 4 (December, 1962), pp. 385-95.

Blum, Arthur, "Values and Aspirations as a Focus for Treatment." *Social Work Practice* (Selected Papers from the National Conference on Social Welfare). New York, Columbia University Press (1963), pp. 31-43.

Buxbaum, Edith, "Transference and Group Formation in Children and Adolescents." *The Psychoanalytic Study of the Child,* Vol. I. New York, International Universities Press, 1945. pp. 351-65.

Chuan, Marian, "Providing a Therapeutic Environment in a Pediatric Service." *Child Welfare,* Vol. XLI, No. 5, May 1962. pp. 219-222.

Conrad, Gertrude, "Development of a Group Counseling Program in a Family Service Agency." *Social Casework* XXXIX, No. 10, October, 1958. pp. 560-564

Corletti, June A., "Group Treatment of Chronic Regressed Psychiatric Patients." *Social Casework,* XLIV, February, 1963.

Eisen A., "Group Work with Newly Arrived Patients in a Mental Hospital" *Social Work with Groups,* National Association of Social Workers, 1958. pp. 94-105.

Eisen, Arnold, Abraham Lurie, and Lewis Robbins, "Group Processes in a Voluntary Hospital." *American Journal of Orthopsychiatry,* XXXIII, No. 4, July, 1963. pp. 750-754.

Elliot, Mabel A., "Group Therapy in Dealing With Juvenile and Adult Offenders." *Federal Probation,* Vol. XXVII, No. 3, December, 1963. pp. 48-54.

Fenton, Norman E., *Explorations in the Use of Group Counseling in the County Correctional Program.* Palo Alto, Pacific Books, 1962.

Frey, Louise A., "Social Group Work in Hospitals."
New Perspectives on Services to Groups: Theory, Organization, Practice. New York, National Association of
Social Workers, 1961. pp. 92-103.

Frey, Louise and Kolodny, Ralph, "Illusions and
Realities in Current Social Work with Groups."
Social Work, IX, No. 2, April, 1964. pp. 80-89.

Funt, Irene, "The Applications of Casework Principles in Family Life Education." *Social Casework,*
Vol. XLIII, No. 3. pp. 130-137.

Ganter, Grace, "The Group Worker in the Child
Guidance Center." *Group Work in the Psychiatric
Setting,* Harleigh B. Treker, ed. New York,
Whiteside and Morrow, 1956.

Ganter, Grace and Polansky, Norman, "Predicting a
Child's Accessibility to Individual Treatment from
Diagnostic Groups" IX, No. 3, July, 1964.
Social Work, 56-63.

Grunwald, Hannah, "Group Counseling with the
Multi Problem Family." *Use of Group Techniques
in the Family Agency.* New York, Family Service
Association of America, 1959.

86

Gump, Paul, "Observational Study of Activities for Disturbed Children." *Group Work and Community Organization, 1953-54.* New York, Columbia University Press, 1954. pp. 12-22.

Gump, Paul, "The 'It' Role in Children's Games." *The Group,* XVIII, February, 1955. pp. 3-8.

Harlow, Minnie Maude, "Group Work in a Psychiatric Hospital," National Conference on Social Welfare, *Mental Health and Social Welfare.* New York, Columbia University Press, 1961. pp. 152-74.

Heldoorn, Jean, "Social Group Work in a Multidiscipline Resident Institution." *Social Work with Groups, 1959.* pp. 82-95.

Irons, Lucia and Ganter, Grace, "The Co-ordination of Group Work and Casework to Promote Effective Treatment in a Child Guidance Clinic." *The American Journal of Orthopsychiatry,* XXV, January, 1955. pp. 138-47.

Jones, John H., "Group Work with Delinquent Adolescent Boys." *Social Work with Groups, 1959.* pp. 66-81.

Kaplan, Irving H., "Some Aspects of Group Work in a Psychiatric Setting." *Social Work, V,* July, 1960. pp. 84-90.

Kolodny, Ralph L., "A Group Work Approach to the Isolated Child." *Social Work, VI,* July, 1961. pp. 76-84.

Kolodny, Ralph L., "Therapeutic Group Work with Handicapped Children." *Children, IV,* No. 3, May-June, 1957. pp. 95-101.

Kraft, Irvin A., "Some Special Considerations in Adolescent Group Psychotherapy." *International Journal of Group Psychotherapy XI,* No. 2, April, 1961. pp. 196-203.

Lerman, Paul, "Group Work with Youth in Conflict." *Social Work III,* October, 1958. pp. 71-77.

MacLennan, Beryce W., "Group Treatment of the Unmarried Mother" in *Casework Papers, 1954.* New York, Family Service Association of America, 1954. pp. 116-30.

Matsushima, John, "Group Work with Emotionally Disturbed Children in Residential Treatment." *Social Work,* VII, No. 2, April, 1962. pp. 62-70.

McCoy, Jacqueline and Donahue, Jack M., "Educating Foster Mothers Through The Group Process." *Child Welfare,* X, No. 3, March, 1961.

Middleman, Ruth, "Social Group Work in a Maternity Home." *Child Welfare,* February, 1959. pp. 13-18.

Morgan, Patricia M., "A Project on Resocialization of Patients in a Mental Hospital, Use of Group Work Techniques." *Social Casework,* Vol. XLII, No. 2. pp. 60-65.

Morse, William C. and Small, Edna R., "Group Life Space Interviewing in a Therapeutic Camp." *Journal of Orthopsychiatry,* XXIX, January, 1959. pp. 27-44.

Nadel, Robert, "A Counseling Program for Parents of Severely Retarded Preschool Children." *Social Case Work,* Vol. XLII, No. 2, February, 1961. pp. 78-83.

Northen, Helen, "Social Group Work: A Tool for Changing Behavior of Disturbed Acting-out Adolescents." *Social Work with Groups,* 1958. pp. 61-74.

Ohlin, Lloyd E., and Lawrence, William C., "Social Interaction Among Clients as a Treatment Problem." *Social Work,* IV, April, 1959. pp. 3-13.

Ortoff, Murray, "Group Services to Families Receiving ADC." *Child Welfare,* XLI, No. 3, March, 1962.

Osborne, Hazel, "Some Factors of Resistance Which Affect Group Participation." *Readings in Group Work,* Dorothy Sullivan, ed. New York, Association Press, 1952. pp. 1-24.

Pavenstedt, Eleanor, M.D., "A Child Guidance Service in a Municipal Hospital." *Children,* X, No. 6, 1963. pp. 207-12.

Peince, F. J., "Social Group Work in a Women's Prison." *Federal Probation,* Vol. XXVII, No. 4, December, 1963. pp. 37-43.

Pollok, Gertrude, "Family Life Education for Parents of Acting Out Children." *Journal of Marriage and Family,* XXVI, No. 4, November, 1964.

Prange, Francis B., "The Self Improvement Group at the McNeil Island Penitentiary." *Federal Probation,* Vol. XXVII, No. 1, March, 1963. pp. 34-36.

Rogers, Muriel N., "A Group Educational Program for Marginally Adjusted Families." *Social Casework,* Vol. XLIII, No. 4. pp. 178-184.

Redl, Fritz, "The Therapeutic Ingredients in the Group Work Program in a Residential Treatment Center," in *Group Work in the Psychiatric Setting,* Harleigh B. Trecker, ed. New York, Whiteside and Morrow, 1956. pp. 43-48.

Richards, Catherine, "Finding a Focus for Work with Hostile Youth Groups." *Social Work with Groups, 1958.* pp. 75-86.

Shoemaker, Louise P., "Social Group Work in the ADC Program." *Social Work,* VIII, No. 1, January, 1963. pp. 30-36.

Shoemaker, Louise P., "Use of Group Work Skills with Short-Term Groups." *Social Work with Groups, 1960.* pp. 37-51.

Soffeen, Joseph, "The Impact of a Group Educational Program for Foster Parents." *Child Welfare,* Vol. XLI, No. 2, May, 1962.

Songes, Kathleen, "A Geriatric Counseling Group." *Social Work,* Vol. 7, No. 4, October, 1962. pp. 61-65.

Stanley, Ruth Light, "The Group Method in Foster Home Studies." *Social Work Practice Selected Papers: National Conference on Social Welfare.* New York, Columbia University Press, 1963. pp. 221-34.

Steidemann, Elthea, "Group Treatment with Resistive Clients." *Social Casework,* XLV, No. 1, January, 1964. pp. 26-31.

Tanaka, Henry, "Group Living on a Psychiatric Ward." *Social Work,* VII, No. 4, October, 1962. pp. 51-58.

Thomas, Carolyn, "The Use of Group Methods with Foster Parents." *Children,* VIII, No. 6, November-December, 1961. pp. 218-22.

Tolman, Norman G., "Approaching the Institutionalized Female Delinquent Through Group Therapy." *Federal Probation,* Vol. XXV, No. 2, June, 1961. pp. 34-40.

Trecker, Harleigh, ed., *Group Services in Public Welfare* (Guides for Adminstration and Program Development). Washington, D. C., U. S. Department of Health, Education, and Welfare (Bureau of Family Services), 1964. (Monograph.)

Weiner, Hyman J., "The Hospital, The Ward and the Patient as Clients: Use of the Group Method." *Social Work,* IV, October, 1959. pp. 57-64.

Wiltse, Kermit, and Fenton, Norman, eds., *Group Methods in the Public Welfare Program.* Palo Alto, California, Pacific Books.

Woodruff, Robert, "Group Work in a Children's Hospital." *Social Work,* II, No. 3, July, 1957. pp. 56-61.

Young, Carol, "Social Group Work with Children in a General Hospital." *Group Work Papers, 1957.* New York, N.A.S.W. pp. 50-61.

Youngman, Louise, "Social Group Work in the AFDC Program." *Public Welfare.* January, 1965. pp. 25-31, 59-61.